See Christ at Christmas:
A 25-day Journey

ERIC DYKSTRA

Thrill & Move
worldwide

Thrill & Move Worldwide
St Paul, Minnesota

See Christ at Christmas: A 25-day Journey
Copyright © 2017 by Eric Dykstra

Cover design by Tracy Keech

ISBN-13: 978-0-9960223-5-4

HOW TO USE THIS DEVOTIONAL

Each day in the month of December leading up to Christmas, read the verse about the birth of Jesus and study how it applies to you.

MY HOPE FOR YOU

I pray that all who study the Savior's birth this Christmas experience Jesus in a real way. May the holidays be more than a tradition. May Christ come alive to each reader and change your life forever. May you encounter the joy of the angels as you read about the love of the Father. God bless you!

December 1

Isaiah 7:14 ...the Lord himself will give you the sign. Look! The virgin will conceive a child! She will give birth to a son and will call him Immanuel (which means 'God is with us').

It took a while, but this prophecy finally came to pass when Jesus was born !

Do you ever feel like the promises of God are not coming to pass for you? We all feel that way at times. We read the Scriptures and see God's promises, but we sometimes struggle to see them fulfilled! Don't lose hope.

In the words of the great theologians Journey: Don't Stop Believing!

Isaiah prophesied the birth of the Messiah in 700 B.C.! The people waited a long time before Jesus finally showed up, but eventually, HE DID! At just the right time, the prophecy was fulfilled and Jesus came to earth to rescue us.

I don't know what you are believing for, but don't get discouraged, and don't lose your hope. Jesus will come through for you at just the right time. It may look like it is taking a while, but God has not forgotten you. Like Jesus showed up at the right time to redeem us, He will show up in your life at just the right time to save you as well! Keep the faith. Keep on believing!

Write down one thing you are believing for today, and then tell God you believe He will come through for you and you will not stop believing.

_____

_____

_____

_____

_____

_____

_____

_____

_____

_____

_____

_____

_____

_____

_____

_____

December 2

Matthew 1:22-23 All of this occurred to fulfill the Lord's message through his prophet: "Look! The virgin will conceive a child! She will give birth to a son, and they will call him Immanuel, which means 'God is with us.'"

What does your name mean? My name, Eric, means "kingly warrior". I love that about myself. I love that I was labeled by my parents as a kingly warrior. My wife Kelly's name means "excellent warrior". We have a peaceful relationship, obviously.

Notice Jesus' name is "Immanuel". The name His Father in Heaven labeled Him with means "God with us."

That is profoundly life-altering for you and me! Jesus doesn't just see us from a distance. He doesn't just observe from the heavens. NO, He came to earth to be with us. You are never alone because of Jesus. YOU will never be forsaken because of Jesus. He is with you through every trial and trouble. He is with you on the good days and on the bad ones. He never gives up on you or abandons you.

No matter what you are going through today, know that Jesus is with you and there for you. He's closer than you think.

Write down one place you have to go today where you know you will need Jesus with you. Ask Him to walk with you through that situation to guide you, comfort you, and protect you.

_____

December 3

Isaiah 9:6 For a child is born to us, a son is given to us. The government will rest on his shoulders. And he will be called: Wonderful Counselor, Mighty God, Everlasting Father, Prince of Peace.

I have several titles. Father. Husband. Pastor. Friend. Fisherman. Like me, Jesus has several titles. The prophet Isaiah wrote down four of them.

He called Him "Wonderful Counselor".

This means when you are internally confused and struggling, you can go to Him with your questions. Like a good counselor, He will guide your steps and give you good wisdom.

He called Him "Mighty God".

This means He is not just a good man, but He is a powerful God. He is strong enough to handle what you are going through. You can trust Him to help you and rescue you because He is mighty.

He called Him "Everlasting Father".

This means Jesus has always existed. Before the world was created, He was there. He is here now with you, and He will be there after the world is gone. Trust that He knows the beginning of your story, the middle, and the end. He has it all worked out and is in total control.

He called Him "Prince of Peace".

This means Jesus is the ruler (or owner) of peace. He alone can bring peace into your heart and life. Pray to Him and ask Him for His supernatural peace. He promises to provide it.

Now that you know His titles, which one means the most to you today? Write it down. Then write out a prayer asking Him for what you need based on that title.

_____

_____

_____

_____

_____

_____

_____

_____

_____

_____

_____

_____

_____

_____

December 4

Micah 5:2 But you, O Bethlehem Ephrathah, are only a small village among all the people of Judah. Yet a ruler of Israel, whose origins are in the distant past, will come from you on my behalf.

Jesus came from a little town called Bethlehem. It was a nothing of a town. Insignificant. Small. Overlooked. But God chose this little town to be the place where Christ was born!

Have you ever felt insignificant? Overlooked? Unimportant? Then you are in good company, because God loves to use the insignificant. He loves to use the overlooked or the forgotten or the abandoned. He loves to use those that feel unimportant. God's specialty is to use the people and places that the world would find less valuable.

Just like God chose Bethlehem, He chooses you. You are perfect for God to use to bring about change in the world!

Go to work or school or wherever you need to go today knowing that He's going to use you for something significant, even if others don't see your significance yet. It'll happen. He's going to use you to change the world for good!

Write down one way in which you will try to be a blessing in the world today. Be the change you want to see. Go let God use you today!

_____
_____
_____
_____
_____
_____
_____
_____
_____
_____
_____
_____
_____
_____
_____
_____
_____
_____
_____
_____
_____
_____

December 5

John 1:14 So the Word [Jesus] became human and made his home among us. He was full of unfailing love and faithfulness. And we have seen his glory, the glory of the Father's one and only Son.

Have you ever wondered if God understands you? I have. Sometimes when I'm going through something difficult, the thought crosses my mind, "Does God really understand what I'm feeling and experiencing? He feels so distant, and I am not really sure He gets it!"

I have felt this. But here is the truth: He does understand us because of Jesus! Jesus (who was and is God) came to earth and became human. The Ruler and Creator of the world floated in the amniotic fluid of a teenage girl's womb. Jesus entrusted Himself to a poor Jewish couple in the middle of nowhere. He gets what it means to be human.

He learned to read, walk, and talk. He went through the struggle of being hungry, lonely, angry, and tired. He got sick, and He also fell down and scraped His knee. He went through the weirdness of puberty, and, at some point, probably felt the tension of attraction to a woman.

He went through everything you and I go through. This means JESUS UNDERSTANDS! He understands our struggles and problems, He relates to our weaknesses, and He feels our pain.

You have a God who gets it.

Today, write down one thing that is hard or painful that you are going through. Then write down a prayer thanking Jesus that He understands it, is with you in it, and will help you through it.

_____
_____
_____
_____
_____
_____
_____
_____
_____
_____
_____
_____
_____
_____
_____
_____
_____
_____
_____
_____

December 6

Philippians 2:6-8 Though he was God, he did not think of equality with God as something to cling to. Instead, he gave up his divine privileges; he took the humble position of a slave and was born as a human being. When he appeared in human form, he humbled himself in obedience to God and died a criminal's death on a cross.

When Jesus was born and placed in the manger on Christmas Day, He was giving up His rights to control the universe. He was God, but when He became a human, He was not laying there thinking God thoughts in the manger. He was not laying there thinking, "I am the ultimate cosmic power controlling the universe, from inside a tiny baby." No! He was laying in the manger thinking baby thoughts. Goo goo, gaga, etc.

Pastor Eric, why are you telling me this? Because I want you to understand that Jesus gave up His divine privileges to be with YOU. He was God, and He had everything except you. And so He came to earth to be with you out of love. He gave up everything - like a royal prince giving up the crown and all its privileges - to be with the ones He loves. This is Jesus' love for you.

Today, will you love Him back?

Take a second and write out a prayer of commitment, telling Jesus that you love Him, that you are thankful for Him, and that you will serve Him in whichever ways He needs.

_____

_____

_____

_____

_____

_____

_____

_____

_____

_____

_____

_____

_____

_____

_____

_____

_____

_____

_____

_____

_____

_____

_____

_____

_____

_____

_____

_____

December 7

Matthew 1:1, 3, 5-6 This is a record of the ancestors of Jesus the Messiah, a descendant of David and of Abraham: Judah was the father of Perez and Zerah (<u>whose mother was Tamar</u>). Perez was the father of Hezron. Hezron was the father of Ram. Salmon was the father of Boaz (<u>whose mother was Rahab</u>). Boaz was the father of Obed (<u>whose mother was Ruth</u>). Obed was the father of Jesse. Jesse was the father of King David. David was the father of Solomon (<u>whose mother was Bathsheba</u>, the widow of Uriah).

I gave you part of the lineage of Jesus today. I kind of jumped around a bit because I wanted you to see who the grandmothers and great-grandmothers of Jesus were.

Why am I pointing this out? Two reasons:

First, in ancient culture, only the men are listed in a genealogy. God values women equally with men. Just had to throw that out there.

Second, the four women listed here are some interesting characters. They are kind of the bad girls of the Bible.

- Tamar slept with her father-in-law.
- Rahab was a prostitute.
- Ruth was an outsider who worshipped idols.
- Bathsheba was an adulteress who slept with King David!

The Bible includes these four women for a profound reason. I think God is saying, "I choose to use jacked-up people to accomplish My purposes. These women were not perfect little nice girls. In fact, they were pretty rough-around-the-edges. But I chose them to be the grandmothers of the Savior of mankind!"

Wow! That's awesome! Don't think you are too jacked-up to be in the family of God. Don't think you are too far gone to be used by God. Don't ever think your mistakes keep God from wanting to draw close to you. He loves you in spite of your weaknesses. He wants you in His family, no matter your mistakes. He desires to use you for something good in the world, despite your past.

Today, write down a prayer of gratitude that Jesus loves you in spite of your weaknesses. Tell Him thank you that He wants you in His family!

_____

_____

_____

_____

_____

_____

_____

December 8

Matthew 1:18 This is how Jesus the Messiah was born. His mother, Mary, was engaged to be married to Joseph. But before the marriage took place, while she was still a virgin, she became pregnant through the power of the Holy Spirit.

Here is what I believe this verse teaches us - God uses ordinary people to accomplish extraordinary things.

Mary was just a teenage girl. Joseph was just a carpenter. But in the hands of God and the power of the Holy Spirit, these two ordinary people became extraordinary.

Never underestimate how a natural act of kindness can supernaturally affect the world.

Never underestimate your ability to be used by the Holy Spirit to accomplish something extraordinary.

Never underestimate how a positive word can affect a life forever.

We live in a natural world, but the supernatural breaks through every time we allow God to use us.

Today, ask the Holy Spirit to open doors. Ask Him to use you to do something good in the world or speak a blessing over someone else. Like God used ordinary Mary and Joseph, God will use ordinary you if you will invite Him to.

_____

_____

_____

_____

_____

_____

_____

_____

_____

_____

_____

_____

_____

_____

_____

_____

_____

_____

_____

_____

_____

_____

December 9

Matthew 1:19-21 Joseph, to whom she was engaged, was a righteous man and did not want to disgrace her publicly, so he decided to break the engagement quietly. As he considered this, an angel of the Lord appeared to him in a dream. "Joseph, son of David," the angel said, "do not be afraid to take Mary as your wife. For the child within her was conceived by the Holy Spirit. And she will have a son, and you are to name him Jesus, for he will save his people from their sins."

There are two things I want you to notice from this passage today:

1. God will guide you if you are open to being led. Notice, God spoke to Joseph in the dream. The Scriptures say that God speaks to those who are in his flock (John 10:27). If you are a child of God, God wants to guide your steps today. Like Joseph, you must be open to listening to His voice.

2. Christ's primary purpose on earth was to save His people from their sins. Jesus' mission was to pay the price for your mistakes and bad choices. Never forget that salvation is free, but it wasn't cheap. Jesus paid a high price to save you. He

died in your place. The child in the manger was headed for the cross.

Here is a suggested application. Write down one thing and then do one thing today:

1. Write down one area about which you need Jesus to speak to you and guide your steps this week.

2. Tell Him thank you for dying for you and saving you from your sins by taking communion. Go get a little bit of wine or juice and some crackers and eat and drink, thanking Jesus for His sacrifice for you!

_____
_____
_____
_____
_____
_____
_____
_____
_____
_____
_____
_____
_____
_____
_____

December 10

Matthew 1:24-25 When Joseph woke up, he did as the angel of the Lord commanded and took Mary as his wife. But he did not have sexual relations with her until her son was born. And Joseph named him Jesus.

When Joseph woke up from his dream, the Scriptures say he did what the angel told him to do. Boom. Obedience.

When God tells us something, we need to immediately obey it. We don't obey because we have to, we obey because we get to participate in the supernatural! When we disobey God, we miss out on all that He has planned to accomplish through us! So obey Him! Joseph enjoyed the privilege of being the earthly father of Jesus simply because he obeyed what God said!

What has God already told you to do, that you just haven't done?

- Forgive someone? You are missing out on the supernatural!
- Become generous and tithe? You are missing out on the supernatural!
- Read your Bible daily? You are missing out on the supernatural!

Maybe the reason why you never experience God is because you just didn't do the last thing He told you to do. Go and do it! God has supernatural great things for you.

Write down one thing God has told you to do that you have not done yet. Then tell God you are sorry, and go and do it today. Don't wait any longer.

_____
_____
_____
_____
_____
_____
_____
_____
_____
_____
_____
_____
_____
_____
_____
_____
_____
_____
_____
_____
_____
_____

December 11

Matthew 2:1-2 Jesus was born in Bethlehem in Judea, during the reign of King Herod. About that time some wise men from eastern lands arrived in Jerusalem, asking, "Where is the newborn king of the Jews? We saw his star as it rose, and we have come to worship him."

We believe that the wise men probably came from around Babylon. It wasn't convenient, and it wasn't easy. They had to study what the star meant. They had to travel hundreds of miles over desert. They had to talk to dangerous kings like Herod. All to find Jesus.

I need to tell you, seeking Jesus is not always easy. It's not always convenient. Sometimes it can be very difficult and challenging. But wise people still seek Him.

They study Him in His Word.

They meditate on His teaching.

They come to worship, though it is not always convenient.

If you were to look at your life right now, are you wise? Are you seeking Him in His Word? Are you meditating on His teaching? Are you coming to worship, even if it's not convenient? Very simply, you know if you are moving toward wisdom if those three things can be said of you.

Today, maybe you could change. Today, maybe you could gain wisdom by actually seeking Jesus. Don't just say you believe in Him - seek Him.

Challenge: go to worship this weekend, even if it is not convenient. Read His Word today, even if you don't have tons of time. Pray to Him and meditate on His Word all throughout your day today.

WISE MEN SEEK HIM!

_____
_____
_____
_____
_____
_____
_____
_____
_____
_____
_____
_____
_____

December 12

Matthew 2:9-11 After this interview the wise men went their way. And the star they had seen in the east guided them to Bethlehem. It went ahead of them and stopped over the place where the child was. When they saw the star, they were filled with joy! They entered the house and saw the child with his mother, Mary, and they bowed down and worshiped him. Then they opened their treasure chests and gave him gifts of gold, frankincense, and myrrh.

The reason why we have a tradition of giving gifts at Christmas is because the wise men brought gifts to Jesus.

They gave Him gold, frankincense, and myrrh.

- Gold speaks of Jesus being King. Gold is a gift for royalty.
- Frankincense speaks of Jesus being our High Priest. Frankincense is an incense priests use in worship.
- Myrrh speaks of Jesus' death for us. It is a burial spice used in the embalming process.

So, what gift are you giving Jesus this Christmas? It is astounding the number of Christians who celebrate

Christmas by giving gifts to everyone else they love (parents, children, spouses), but bring nothing to Jesus. Jesus gave us everything. Our ability to buy gifts for others is because of His goodness to us. Don't forget to give Jesus a significant gift this Christmas.

He deserves your worship. The wise men worshipped by bringing gifts.

Take a minute and prayerfully consider what gift you will bring to Jesus this Christmas. Maybe write a significant check to a church or Christian ministry to say thank you to God for all that Jesus has done for you this year.

Write down the amount and to which area of His Kingdom you are giving a gift in order to worship Jesus this Christmas season.

_____

_____

_____

_____

_____

_____

_____

_____

_____

_____

_____

_____

_____

December 13

Revelation 12:3-5 And another sign appeared in heaven: behold, a great, fiery red dragon having seven heads and ten horns, and seven diadems on his heads. His tail drew a third of the stars of heaven and threw them to the earth. And the dragon stood before the woman who was ready to give birth, to devour her Child as soon as it was born. She bore a male Child who was to rule all nations with a rod of iron. And her Child was caught up to God and His throne. (NKJV)

This is a weird Christmas story. Instead of shepherds and wise men, there's a dragon trying to eat a baby and stars being thrown to the earth and rods of iron. What?!

This is the supernatural side of Christmas. God looks at earth and realizes it is being held hostage by the great dragon, the devil. So He invades. He parachutes into enemy territory as a baby to rescue us. It's like the D-Day invasion! And when He parachutes in, the great dragon, Satan, attacked like the Nazis in an effort to destroy Jesus. Satan influences King Herod to kill all the baby boys in Bethlehem to try and stop Christ's advance. But the devil loses!

Jesus was caught up to heaven and to the throne of God. He will rule with an iron scepter, and there is nothing the devil can do about it.

Jesus wins. Evil loses.

Though it looked like the dragon was going to triumph, he was defeated at the cross. Though it looked like Satan was winning, his defeat was sealed when Jesus rose again and was caught up to heaven.

What does this mean for us? So much!

Heaven invaded earth to rescue you. You were held captive by sin, but Jesus' birth was the first battle to bring you freedom. His mission and sacrifice won the battle for you.

Just as we say thank you to our military veterans for defending our freedom, remember to thank the ultimate Veteran and tell Him you are grateful He won the battle for your freedom.

Write down a prayer of thanksgiving and tell Jesus thank you for invading earth for you.

_____

_____

_____

_____

_____

_____

_____

December 14

Galatians 4:4-5 But when the fullness of the time had come, God sent forth His Son, born of a woman, born under the law, to redeem those who were under the law, that we might receive the adoption as sons. (NKJV)

Jesus came at just the right time to redeem us from the law. What this means is that God knew we were incapable of living up to the high standards of the law. All of us fell short. We continued to lie, cheat, steal, and worship false gods.

God sent Jesus at just the right time. He fulfilled the law perfectly. He did not lie, cheat, or steal. He did not commit adultery or hate or covet. He never worshipped a false God or lusted after a woman. He was perfect in thought, word, and action. That's amazing! He fulfilled the law.

Why? So that we could be adopted into God's family. He was our representative. If we worship Jesus and follow Jesus, God credits Jesus' good works of following the law to us. If we are in Christ, we are adopted into God's family, even though we failed to keep the law. Jesus kept it for us.

Are you trying to earn God's approval today? You already have it because of Jesus! What if today you said thank you to Jesus for fulfilling the law for you? Write out a prayer thanking God for sending Jesus to do what you could not do for yourself. Thank Jesus for being perfect and then giving you credit for His righteousness (2 Corinthians 5:21).

_____

_____

_____

_____

_____

_____

_____

_____

_____

_____

_____

_____

_____

_____

_____

_____

_____

_____

_____

_____

_____

_____

_____

December 15

Luke 1:26-28 In the sixth month of Elizabeth's pregnancy, God sent the angel Gabriel to Nazareth, a village in Galilee, to a virgin named Mary. She was engaged to be married to a man named Joseph, a descendant of King David. Gabriel appeared to her and said, "Greetings, favored woman! The Lord is with you!"

The angel told Mary she was favored, and God was with her! The same can be said for you. If you are a follower of Jesus, you have His favor always. His hand is on your life. He is always with you.

I'm sure there were seasons in Mary's life when Mary doubted this. There must've been times when she really struggled with whether or not she was favored and God was truly with her. But it was true. And she had to believe it to keep moving forward.

The same is true for you and me. There will be seasons in life where we will struggle to believe we are favored and God is with us. But it is true. We will have to believe it in order to keep moving forward.

Today I want you to say out loud, "I am highly favored, and God is with me."

Say it again out loud, and then add another sentence.

"I am highly favored, and God is with me. Circumstances cannot keep the favor of God from me. God is attracted to blessing me, and I will see the goodness of the Lord."

Keep saying it every day. This is the truth. And the truth will set you free.

_____
_____
_____
_____
_____
_____
_____
_____
_____
_____
_____
_____
_____
_____
_____
_____
_____
_____
_____
_____
_____
_____

December 16

Luke 1:30-33 "Don't be afraid, Mary," the angel told her, "for you have found favor with God! You will conceive and give birth to a son, and you will name him Jesus. He will be very great and will be called the Son of the Most High. The Lord God will give him the throne of his ancestor David. And he will reign over Israel forever; his Kingdom will never end!"

Sometimes it feels like God's Kingdom is ending instead of never-ending. It feels like evil is winning in the world, doesn't it? When you hear about tragedy, terrorism, disease, or pain, it's hard to feel like Jesus' Kingdom will never end.

But here's the truth: Satan lost when Jesus rose from the dead. The death and resurrection of Jesus was Satan's loss, so evil cannot win. He has already been judged, and will eventually see that loss become his permanent reality.

Our job is to believe in spite of tragedy and terrorism and disease and pain. Believe that God is good and that He will win in the end. Don't let the darkness of sadness, discouragement, despair, or hopelessness get in your mind or heart. Jesus wins! He beat sin and death. We have already read the end of the Bible, and we know He wins in the end.

There will come a day where we will kneel before the throne and shout, "King of Kings and Lord of Lords!" The Prince of Peace will rule, and there will be no more tragedy or terrorism or disease or pain.

His Kingdom can not and will not end.

Take a second and write down your biggest pain, hopelessness, or discouragement right now, and then write right over it in big letters JESUS WINS. Scribble JESUS WINS over the top of your struggle. Let this reminder empower you as you move forward today.

_____

_____

_____

_____

_____

_____

_____

_____

_____

_____

_____

_____

_____

_____

_____

_____

_____

December 17

Luke 1:35, 37 And the angel answered and said to her, "The Holy Spirit will come upon you, and the power of the Highest will overshadow you... [the] Holy One who is to be born will be called the Son of God. For with God nothing will be impossible." (NKJV)

Nothing is impossible for God. Remember who is on your side.

You have the One who can calm storms with a word.

You have the One who can walk on water.

You have the One that can open the eyes of the blind.

You have the One that can heal the sick and drive out demons.

Nothing is impossible with Jesus.

I know many times your situation feels impossible, but God sent us Someone who can do the impossible. Nothing is too hard for Him. Death could not hold Him. The grave could not keep Him. Satan could not stop Him. He is more powerful than any disease, sickness, addiction, or struggle. Nothing is too hard for

Him. Jesus is in your corner and ready to help. Just trust Him today.

Today, tell God you believe nothing is impossible for Him. Ask Jesus to conquer the struggle that you face. Tell Him you believe He can do it. Write it out as a prayer.

_____

_____

_____

_____

_____

_____

_____

_____

_____

_____

_____

_____

_____

_____

_____

_____

_____

_____

_____

_____

_____

_____

_____

December 18

Luke 1:38 And Mary said, "Behold, I am the servant of the Lord; <u>let it be</u> to me according to your word." And the angel departed from her. (ESV)

The Beatles ripped off the Virgin Mary. Yep, you heard that right. It was Mary who first said, "Let it be."

What Mary was saying was, "God, whatever You want to do with me is OK with me." She was saying, "Whatever You ask of me, I'm in. Wherever You take me, I'll go. Let it be."

I believe she taught those words to her Son as well. When Jesus was in the garden on the night before He died, He said to God, "Not My will, but Yours be done." He was just quoting what His mama had taught Him to say, and to believe.

Parents, don't ever forget that you are teaching your kids what to say and what to believe. They are watching you. Mary taught Jesus to say, "Let it be." His mother taught Him how to handle tough situations. He watched her life. He saw how she responded.

Your kids are watching you. You can teach them to overcome if you will begin to speak faith like Mary.

Begin to say things like, "Let it be to me as You have said." Begin to say things like, "Not my will, but Yours be done." Speak faith.

When this is how you respond to challenges, your kids will learn this pattern and respond this way as well. You will watch them succeed because you taught them to speak faith and trust the Savior.

Write down one area where you need to say, "Let it be," or, "Not my will but yours be done." Pick an area that you can talk to your kids about. Then go tell them how you are trusting God by faith with something difficult. They need to see you still trust Jesus in your vulnerability. Speak faith with them.

_____

_____

_____

_____

_____

_____

_____

_____

_____

_____

_____

_____

_____

_____

_____

December 19

Luke 2:4-7 And because Joseph was a descendant of King David, he had to go to Bethlehem in Judea, David's ancient home. He traveled there from the village of Nazareth in Galilee. He took with him Mary, to whom he was engaged, who was now expecting a child. And while they were there, the time came for her baby to be born. She gave birth to her firstborn son. She wrapped him snugly in strips of cloth and laid him in a manger, because there was no lodging available for them.

Jesus was born in a stable - probably a cave. He was wrapped in strips of cloth and then laid in a cattle trough... a manger.

This is not how you'd expect the King of Kings to be born. You'd expect a parade and a light show and a giant dance party in a palace! But instead, Jesus came in humility. He did not force Himself on the world; He did not make anyone believe. He did not try to twist anyone's arm. He showed up humbly, quietly, and simply.

Sometimes it is good to remember Jesus wasn't trying to impress anyone when He showed up. As Christians, maybe it's time we stop trying so hard to impress others. God will accomplish what He wants to through us. We don't need to try to force our way into situations. God is on our side. He will open doors for us. We can be humble and don't need to brag on ourselves. Part of faith is resting in the truths that God is in control, He will take good care of us, and He will accomplish what He wants without us stressing out and pushing our own agendas.

Christmas reminds us we can be quiet, simple, and humble. God will take care of us and get us to our destiny.

What is one area of your life into which you have been trying too hard to force your way? It's time to rest and trust Jesus. Write the area down, and tell God you are going to trust His timing and effort and stop working so hard on yourself.

_____

_____

_____

_____

_____

_____

_____

_____

_____

_____

_____

_____

_____

_____

December 20

Luke 2:8-12 That night there were shepherds staying in the fields nearby, guarding their flocks of sheep. Suddenly, an angel of the Lord appeared among them, and the radiance of the Lord's glory surrounded them. They were terrified, but the angel reassured them. "Don't be afraid!" he said. "I bring you good news that will bring great joy to all people. The Savior - yes, the Messiah, the Lord - has been born today in Bethlehem, the city of David! And you will recognize him by this sign: You will find a baby wrapped snugly in strips of cloth, lying in a manger."

On the night Jesus was born, angels excitedly told shepherds about the birth of Jesus! Angels did not want to see mankind miss out on the greatest birth of all time! So they shouted to shepherds, "You need to come see Jesus!"

Are you still excited about Jesus? Who is it that you need to tell about the greatest birth of all time? Who needs to hear about this Savior wrapped in strips of cloth? Don't let them miss out on it. Don't let them miss out on the joy of knowing Jesus and experiencing His love!

Write down the name of someone you will invite to a Christmas service at your church. Take a minute to ask God for boldness for yourself (an openness for your friend). Then text them right now to invite them or call them on the phone and talk to them directly.

_____

Here is a sample text you can use:

Hey, I know you might not be much of a church-goer, and I don't know if you've made plans for Christmas yet. My church is doing a really cool Christmas service that I think will not be half-bad, and I wanted to invite you and your family. Do you guys want to go with us? We can save you seats. I think you might like it!

_____
_____
_____
_____
_____
_____
_____
_____
_____
_____
_____
_____
_____
_____
_____
_____

December 21

Luke 2:13-14 And suddenly there was with the angel a multitude of the heavenly host praising God and saying: "Glory to God in the highest, and on earth peace, goodwill toward men!" (NKJV)

This verse says a multitude of angels shouted glory to God and goodwill toward men. The angels believed it so much, they shouted it!

Sometimes it feels like God is distant or uncaring or not paying attention. I know how you get past those feelings - you shout at the darkness like the angels shouted in the darkness.

You shout, "God has goodwill toward me because of Jesus! God likes me. God's favor is on me. God is for me, not against me - because of Jesus."

You have to speak your faith! When you speak faith, you grow your faith. What you speak about today will grow. If you speak discouragement and feelings of loneliness and isolation, you will feel this more and more. It will grow.

But if you will speak faith and shout at the darkness that God has goodwill for you, faith and joy will grow in your mind and heart, and you will have strength to face today and tomorrow.

Here is my suggestion: today speak over and over again, "God has goodwill toward me!" When something discouraging happens, or something does not go your way, say out loud, "God has goodwill for me because of Jesus!" Shout at the darkness until you feel it.

_____

_____

_____

_____

_____

_____

_____

_____

_____

_____

_____

_____

_____

_____

_____

_____

_____

_____

_____

_____

December 22

Luke 2:15-16 So it was, when the angels had gone away from them into heaven, that the shepherds said to one another, "Let us now go to Bethlehem and see this thing that has come to pass, which the Lord has made known to us." And they came with haste and found Mary and Joseph, and the Babe lying in a manger. (NKJV)

I love the way this translation says the shepherds came with haste.

In other words, they went as fast as they could to Jesus. The same is true for you and me. We need to go with haste to the presence of Jesus.

Every day we need to run to Jesus.

Run with haste to Jesus with whatever you face today. Are you dealing with sickness? Run to Jesus. Are you dealing with addiction? Run to Jesus. Are you dealing with confusion or discouragement? Run as fast as you can to Jesus. The way in which you deal with life or move in a better direction is you go as fast as you can into the presence of Jesus. Tell Him your needs. Sit at His feet and listen. Read His Word. Meditate on His teaching. It is Jesus you need to run to.

Today rather than writing something down, talk to God out loud. Run into His presence and tell Him exactly what you need. Only in His presence will you find His peace.

_____
_____
_____
_____
_____
_____
_____
_____
_____
_____
_____
_____
_____
_____
_____
_____
_____
_____
_____
_____
_____
_____
_____
_____
_____
_____
_____
_____
_____

December 23

Luke 2:17-18 Now when they had seen Him, they <u>made widely known</u> the saying which was told them concerning this Child. And all those who heard it marveled at those things which were told them by the shepherds. (NKJV)

When the shepherds experienced Jesus, they had to tell everyone they knew what had happened and how they had seen Jesus. They could not shut up about what they had seen and heard.

The same is true for us. When we have experienced Christ in a real way, we cannot be silent about Him. We want everyone we know to experience Him as we have and we can not shut up about Him.

Who do you need to talk to about Jesus today? Go and tell them. Don't be silent. Don't shut up. Write down the name of somebody that you need to talk to today about faith.

_____

Commit to inviting them to one of the Christmas services at your church so they can hear the good news of Christ and experience Him for themselves.

December 24

Luke 2:19-20 But Mary <u>kept</u> all these things and <u>pondered</u> them in her heart. Then the shepherds returned, <u>glorifying</u> and <u>praising</u> God for all the things that they had heard and seen, as it was told them. (NKJV)

Merry Christmas Eve! It is almost Christmas! The verse we just read says that after experiencing the birth of Christ, there are two good responses you can have.

Mary was thoughtful and pondered these things in her heart. The Shepherds were vocal, glorifying God and praising Him everywhere they went.

Both of these are good responses to have following an encounter with Christ.

We need moments where we are quiet and ponder all that God has done for us. Don't forget the gospel message is first for you before you start shouting it to others.

Take a minute to be silent this Christmas Eve. Don't just rush through the holiday and forget to pause and reflect on all that Jesus has personally done for you.

Take a few minutes and write down one real way you have experienced Christ this year. Ponder this moment and cherish it. It is a big deal that Jesus has been so good to you!

Secondly, we need to be vocal about how Jesus has changed us and glorify Him to others. Think of one person with whom you can share your story of how Christ has changed you this year. Go share your story with them right now - don't wait. Vocally glorify God and His goodness to them. This might be the thing that nudges that person across the line of faith.

_____
_____
_____
_____
_____
_____
_____
_____
_____
_____
_____
_____
_____
_____
_____
_____
_____
_____

December 25

Matthew 2:12 When it was time to leave, [the wise men] returned to their own country by another route, for God had warned them in a dream not to return to Herod.

Merry Christmas! It is finally Christmas Day. We have studied the Christmas story for 25 days now! How has it changed you?

After the wise men had seen Jesus, they went home a different way. They did not return the same way they came.

Neither can you.

After you have seen Jesus, you can never return the same way you came. You will be changed. You will be different. Once you have experienced Jesus, you go home differently then when you came.

Lots of people come to church and leave the same way they came - because they didn't see Jesus. Many people read the Bible and are left unchanged because they did not see Jesus. Often Christmas comes and goes and we are no different because we failed to see Jesus.

Don't miss out on Christ this Christmas.

Write down one way you will be different because of this 25-day study. You do not want to leave the same way you came!

_____
_____
_____
_____
_____
_____
_____
_____
_____
_____
_____
_____
_____
_____
_____
_____
_____
_____
_____
_____
_____
_____
_____
_____

ABOUT ERIC DYKSTRA

Eric Dykstra is a pastor, teacher, and theology nerd. He grew up in Iowa, and makes his home in St. Paul, Minnesota. He and his wife Kelly founded The Crossing, a multi-site church north of Minneapolis, in 2004. Eric's passions include seeing people cross the line of faith and follow Jesus, fishing for smallmouth bass, and traveling with his family.

Eric is the author of *Grace on Tap* and *Unhooked & Untangled: Finding freedom from your addictions, vices and bad habits.* Both are available on Amazon.

His caffeinated teaching style engages even the most skeptical listeners and inspires people at all stages of faith. You can find his sermons at freegrace.tv or on The Crossing Church smartphone app.

Facebook.com/PastorEricDykstra
Twitter @EricDykstra

72844573R00033

Made in the USA
Lexington, KY
03 December 2017